kids draw™

BABY ANIMALS

CHRISTOPHER HART

WATSON-GUPTILL PUBLICATIONS/NEW YORK

To all my readers—
those who've never read my books before
and those who've come back for more

Senior Editor: Candace Raney
Editors: Alisa Palazzo and Julie Mazur
Designers: Bob Fillie, Graphiti Design, Inc. and Cheryl Viker
Production Manager: Hector Campbell

Front and back cover illustrations by Christopher Hart
Text copyright © 2001 Christopher Hart
Illustrations copyright © 2000 Christopher Hart

First published in 2001 by
Watson-Guptill Publications,
a division of BPI Communications, Inc.,
770 Broadway, New York, N.Y. 10003
www.watsonguptill.com

Based on *How to Draw Cartoon Baby Animals,*
published in 2000 by Watson-Guptill Publications.

Library of Congress Card Number: 00-111763

Printed in Singapore

First printing, 2001

1 2 3 4 5 6/ 06 05 04 03 02 01

CONTENTS

Introduction 5

Baby Animal Basics 6

THE BABY ANIMAL HEAD
THE HEAD IN 3/4 VIEW
THE BABY ANIMAL BODY
ANIMALS THAT WALK LIKE PEOPLE
SITTING ANIMALS
SIMPLE ANIMAL ANATOMY
TYPES OF BABY ANIMAL CHARACTERS
BABY VS. ADULT PROPORTIONS
THE KEYS TO DRAWING A YOUNG ANIMAL

THE PAWS OF VARIOUS SPECIES
DRAWING THE EYES IN PERSPECTIVE
THE SLOPE OF THE FOREHEAD
A FEW TRICKS OF THE TRADE
YOUTHFUL MUZZLES
YOUTHFUL MOUTHS
DRAWING THE FUR
RUFFLES ON THE CHEEKS
BABY ANIMAL EXPRESSIONS

Wild Things! 26

ELEPHANTS
ELEPHANT LEGS
ELEPHANT DETAILS
MONKEYING AROUND
PRIMATE PRIMER
LIONS

TIGERS
HIPPOS
RHINOS
GIRAFFES
ZEBRAS
BEARS

Sea Creatures and Reptiles 40

UNDERWATER YOUNGSTERS
SEALS AND WALRUSES
A WHALE OF A BABY

ALLIGATORS
TURTLES, SNAKES, AND FROGS

Small Cuties 46

BASIC LITTLE BIRDS
PENGUINS (BRR!)
DUCKS

BEAVERS
PIG-OUT!

House Pets and Pests 52

BUNNIES
BUNNIES IN MOTION: BUNCHING AND STRETCHING
HOW MUCH IS THAT DOGGY IN THE WINDOW?
PUREBRED PUPPIES

MUTTS, MUTTS, AND MORE MUTTS!
CUTE LITTLE FUR BALLS
HINTS FOR DRAWING KITTENS
MICE

Index 64

INTRODUCTION

If grownups think that babies are cute, what do kids find adorable? Baby animals, of course! What kid can resist a puppy wagging his tail, tripping over his big floppy ears, and slobbering all over everything? Can you?

Drawing baby animals can be tricky. Babies are not just smaller versions of adults. In fact, they are drawn quite differently. And it's these differences that make baby animals so adorable.

This book will show you how to draw all kinds of baby animals. There are bear, lion, and tiger cubs; baby elephants, rhinos and hippos; bunnies, piglets, and baby birds; beavers, monkeys, dolphins, turtles, frogs, puppies, kittens, and many, many more!

You will also learn an important principle of drawing: how to make your characters look solid and round. This will help bring your drawings to life. So sharpen your pencil, turn the page, and let's have fun!

BABY ANIMAL BASICS

Baby animals are *young* animals, like human babies and children. In the real world, baby animals must grow up quickly to survive. Most learn to walk or swim within mere hours of being born!

The Baby Animal Head

Let's start with the basic baby animal head.

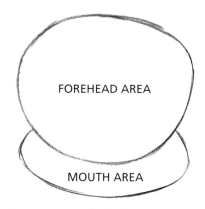

FOREHEAD AREA

MOUTH AREA

The top part of a baby animal head is much bigger than the bottom. This is important to remember.

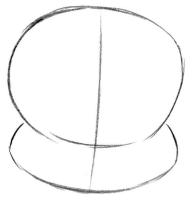

Add a vertical line. This is called the centerline. It divides the head down the middle.

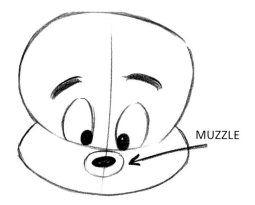

MUZZLE

The eyes go on either side of the centerline. Add eyes and an oval-shaped muzzle (mouth area).

Now add fun stuff, like the smile, the creases of the cheeks, the ears, and the neck. Baby animals either have no neck or a very thin one.

Add some fur, a tongue, whiskers— and you've got it!

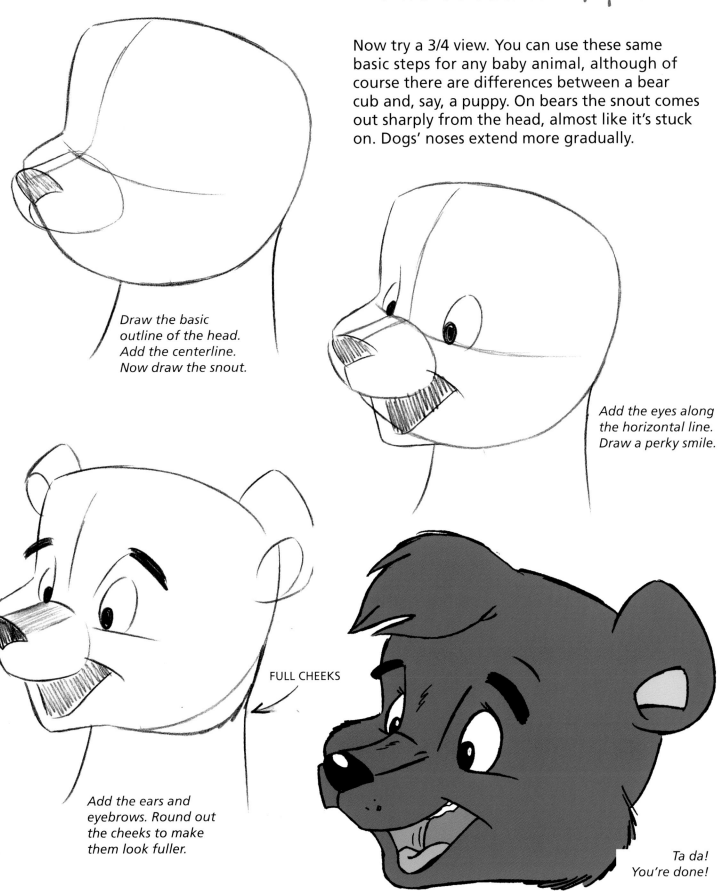

The Head in 3/4 View

Now try a 3/4 view. You can use these same basic steps for any baby animal, although of course there are differences between a bear cub and, say, a puppy. On bears the snout comes out sharply from the head, almost like it's stuck on. Dogs' noses extend more gradually.

Draw the basic outline of the head. Add the centerline. Now draw the snout.

Add the eyes along the horizontal line. Draw a perky smile.

FULL CHEEKS

Add the ears and eyebrows. Round out the cheeks to make them look fuller.

Ta da! You're done!

The Baby Animal Body

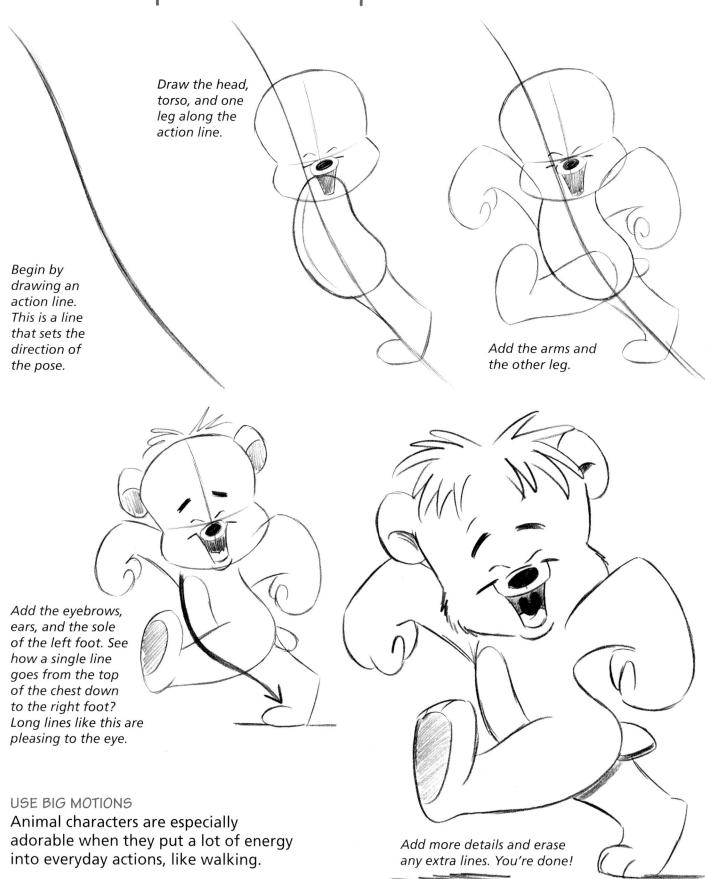

Draw the head, torso, and one leg along the action line.

Begin by drawing an action line. This is a line that sets the direction of the pose.

Add the arms and the other leg.

Add the eyebrows, ears, and the sole of the left foot. See how a single line goes from the top of the chest down to the right foot? Long lines like this are pleasing to the eye.

USE BIG MOTIONS
Animal characters are especially adorable when they put a lot of energy into everyday actions, like walking.

Add more details and erase any extra lines. You're done!

HINDQUARTER

SHOULDER

SIDE VIEW
Even though a baby animal is much smaller than an adult, its body still has some of the same characteristics. A bear cub, for example, has two bumps on its back, just like an adult bear.

3/4 VIEW
Make sure you show the outline of the cub's pudgy tummy. It should overlap the hind legs.

Animals That Walk Like People

Drawing your baby animals upright on two legs—like people—makes them more cartoony.

A face mask separates two colors of fur and highlights the eyes and mouth.

Putting clothes on a young animal can make it even cuter. It will also make your animal more humanlike.

DRAW-THROUGH
You should always draw *all* parts of a figure, even if they will be hidden in the finished drawing. This is called *drawing through.*

Sketch the entire far leg, even though much of it will be hidden in the finished drawing.

Sitting Animals

Baby animal cartoons can also sit upright, like human children.

Claws go in the middle of the edge of the paw, not at the bottom.

A human child leans back when sitting.

A bear cub leans forward.

11

Simple Animal Anatomy

Every animal is supported by a set of bones called the *skeleton.* Knowing the basics of the skeleton will make drawing easier and more fun.

This basic structure works for a horse . . .

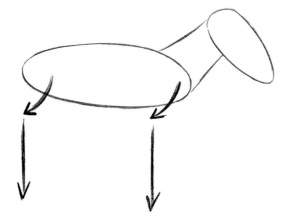

Here's a sketch of your basic four-legged animal. The tops of the legs are short and curve backward (short arrows). The bottoms of the legs are long and straight (long arrows).

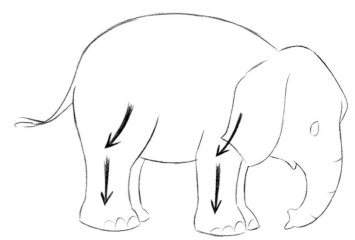

. . . as well as for an elephant . . .

. . . as well as for a rabbit—and many other four-legged creatures.

Types of Baby Animal Characters

In the world of cartoons, there are five basic types of baby animals.

THE GIANT BABY
This bumbling, oversized animal doesn't know his own strength!

THE GOOFY BABY
This cute little critter is a bit on the dizzy side.

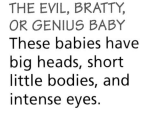

THE LEGGY, AWKWARD BABY
Usually, this is a baby animal with hooves (like a horse or cow), who's off balance on its new legs.

THE WARM AND FUZZY BABY
This one is as cute as a stuffed animal—you just wanna sque-e-e-eze him!

THE EVIL, BRATTY, OR GENIUS BABY
These babies have big heads, short little bodies, and intense eyes.

Baby vs. Adult Proportions

Baby animals are not just smaller versions of adults. They have different types of bodies. Just look at these two horses. The adult's neck is thicker compared to its head. Its muscles are larger. The young horse is bonier. Its hooves are bigger compared to its legs. Its mane is floppier.

The Keys to Drawing a Young Animal

Here are some general points to watch for when drawing a baby animal.

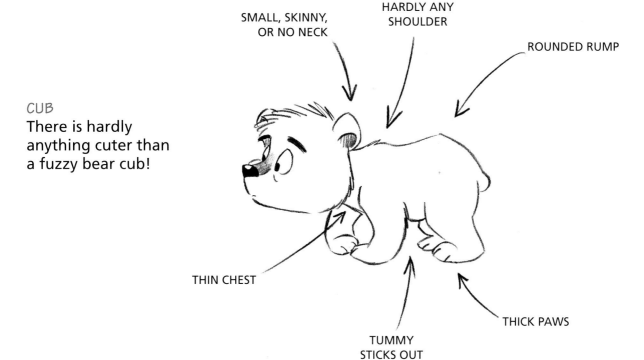

SMALL, SKINNY, OR NO NECK

HARDLY ANY SHOULDER

ROUNDED RUMP

CUB
There is hardly anything cuter than a fuzzy bear cub!

THIN CHEST

TUMMY STICKS OUT

THICK PAWS

ADULT
Notice the powerful neck, huge shoulder hump, and thin paws. The posture is also different.

The Paws of Various Species

Lots of people have trouble drawing hands, or, in this case, paws. Luckily, hind paws are basically the same as front paws. Here are some paws for you to practice.

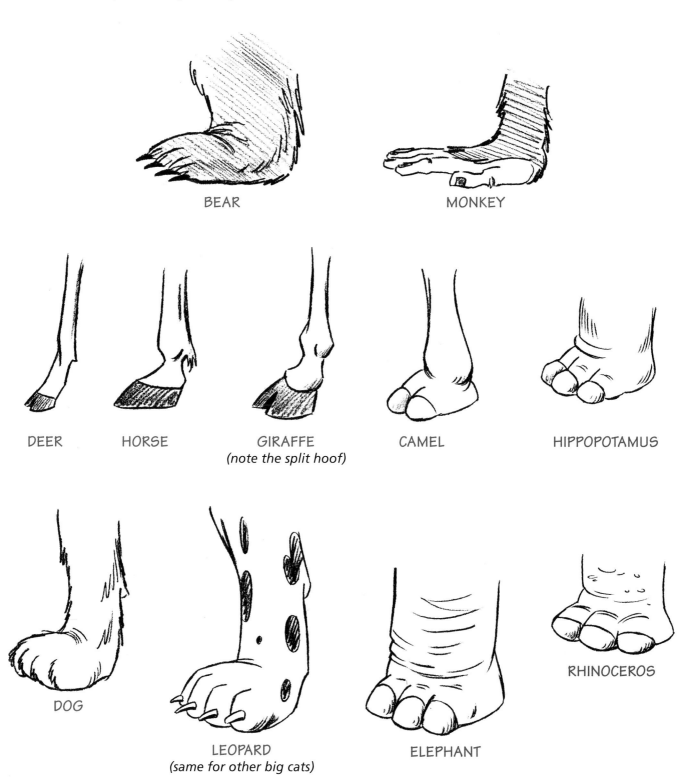

BEAR

MONKEY

DEER

HORSE

GIRAFFE
(note the split hoof)

CAMEL

HIPPOPOTAMUS

DOG

LEOPARD
(same for other big cats)

ELEPHANT

RHINOCEROS

Drawing the Eyes in Perspective

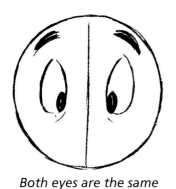

Both eyes are the same size in the front view.

Objects closer to us look larger than objects farther away. This is the rule of *perspective.* Look at the examples of eyes below. In all but one of them, the closer eye is bigger and the farther eye is smaller. When looking straight ahead, the eyes are the same size because they are the same distance away.

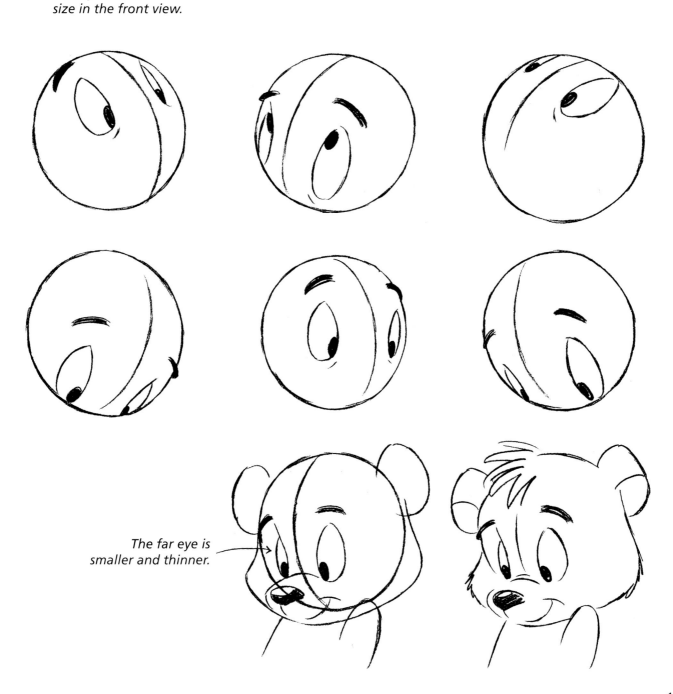

The far eye is smaller and thinner.

The Slope of the Forehead

Here's a good tip to remember. The forehead of a baby animal should be rounded. It should slide gently down the top of the nose in an easy, graceful curve.

The forehead flows down to the top of the nose.

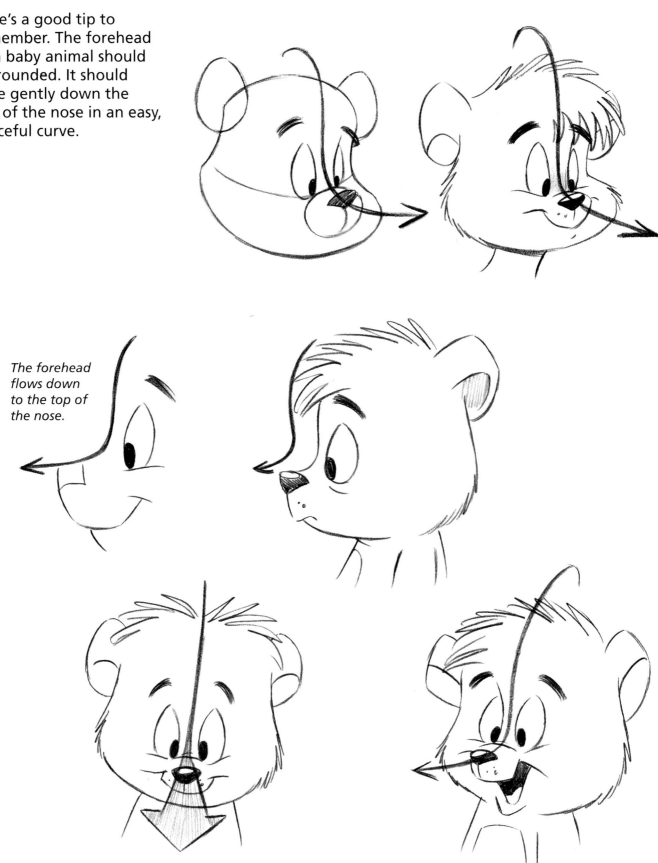

Here are a few more things to keep in mind.

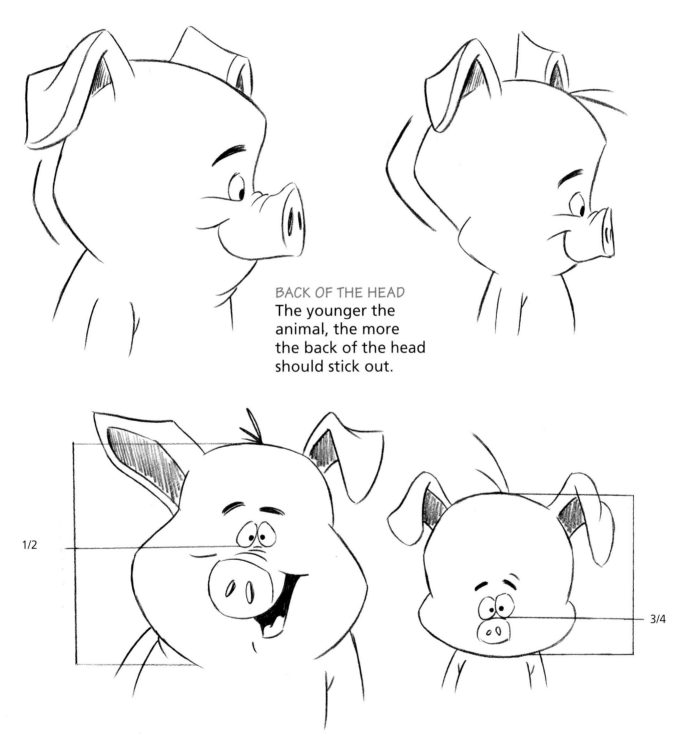

BACK OF THE HEAD
The younger the animal, the more the back of the head should stick out.

1/2

3/4

PLACING THE EYES
The younger the animal, the lower the eyes should be.
Notice how the pig's eyes are only halfway down its head.
The piglet's eyes are 3/4 of the way down.

Youthful Muzzles

The muzzle is the entire mouth, nose, and jaw area. Long muzzles are for adults; short muzzles are for youngsters. The younger the animal, the smaller the chin.

LONG MUZZLE

SHORT MUZZLE

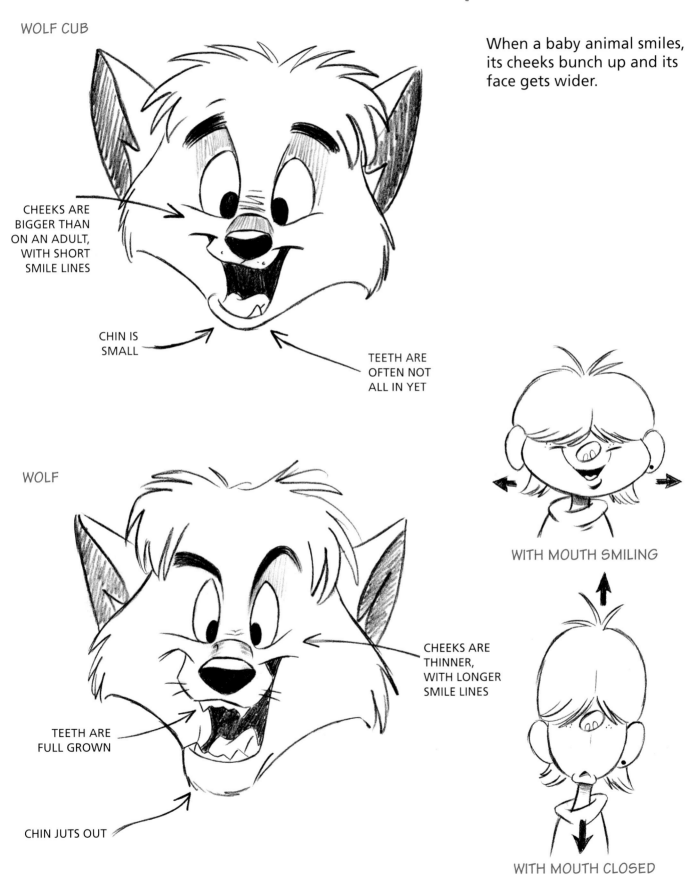

WOLF CUB

When a baby animal smiles, its cheeks bunch up and its face gets wider.

CHEEKS ARE BIGGER THAN ON AN ADULT, WITH SHORT SMILE LINES

CHIN IS SMALL

TEETH ARE OFTEN NOT ALL IN YET

WOLF

WITH MOUTH SMILING

CHEEKS ARE THINNER, WITH LONGER SMILE LINES

TEETH ARE FULL GROWN

CHIN JUTS OUT

WITH MOUTH CLOSED

Drawing the Fur

Drawing ruffles of fur can be tricky. But never fear! Here are some secrets for getting the fur just right.

BEST PLACES FOR RUFFLES OF FUR
Here's your basic kitten. The arrows show which areas should have ruffles. Most animals follows this example.

TOP OF HEAD

INNER EARS

CHEEKS

TIP OF TAIL

CHIN (EVEN A SMALL ONE)

CHEST

RUFFLES FOR DIFFERENT SPECIES
Here are a few tips for specific animals.

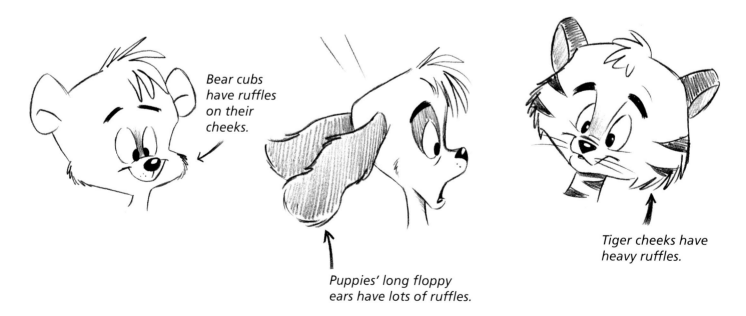

Bear cubs have ruffles on their cheeks.

Puppies' long floppy ears have lots of ruffles.

Tiger cheeks have heavy ruffles.

22

Ruffles on the Cheeks

So how exactly do you draw fur ruffles on the cheeks? Let's look at some examples.

RUFFLES ALL THE WAY AROUND IN ONE DIRECTION
This makes the animal look too furry, almost wild. Plus, the ruffles on one side look upside down.

RUFFLES MEETING IN THE MIDDLE
Again, this looks too furry.

RUFFLES ON EACH CHEEK
This is the best way to draw ruffles, with a long straight line connecting them under the chin.

Baby Animal Expressions

Try drawing your characters from different angles.
Keep their eyes big and bright.

SURPRISED

JOYFUL

MISCHIEVOUS

LAUGHING

GROSSED OUT

SAD

DREAMY

CURIOUS

WILD THINGS!

Elephants, monkeys, lions, tigers, and more! Cute, cuddly animal toddlers are everywhere—even in the most dangerous spots on earth.

Elephants

Elephants have a very limited range of motion. They have no necks, so they have to turn their entire bodies around to look in another direction. They can't run, but can only walk very fast in a weird sort of trot. The elephant's trunk, on the other hand, is very flexible. It can turn and twist in any direction.

Elephant Legs

Long legs on elephants? You betcha! Elephants are actually long-legged animals. Still, there's nothing wrong with giving your elephant short legs if that's what you want.

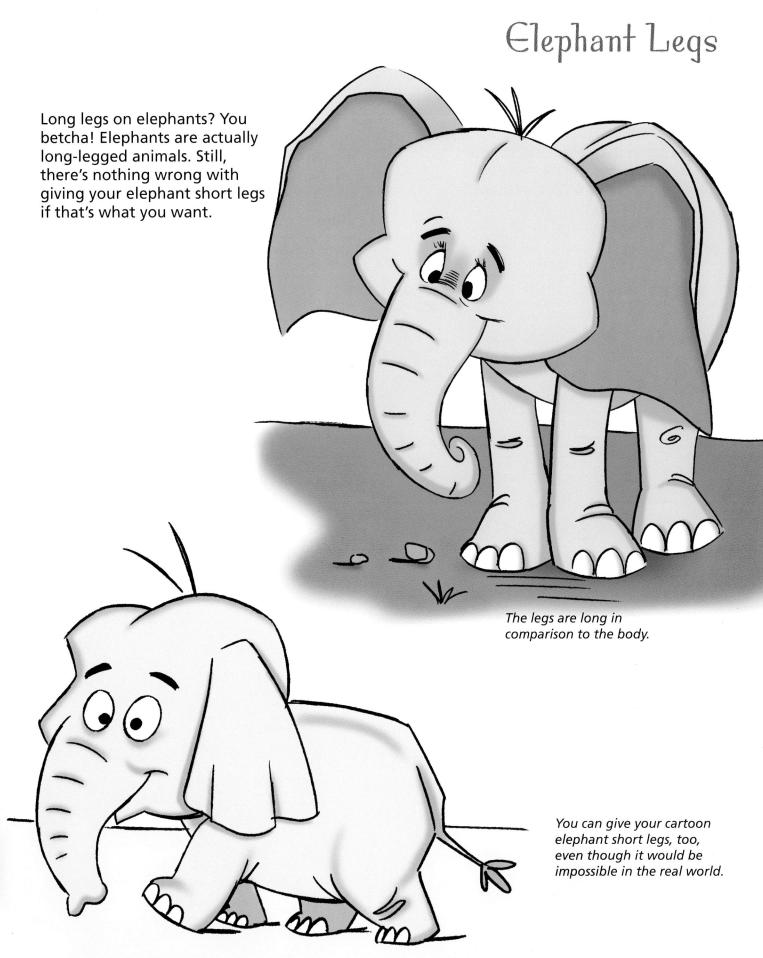

The legs are long in comparison to the body.

You can give your cartoon elephant short legs, too, even though it would be impossible in the real world.

Elephant Details

HAIR

Hair? On an elephant? Yep, and why not? It's a cartoon! More hair makes an animal seem younger. An extra-bushy head of hair makes this little guy look like a tyke, perhaps even a mastodon tyke. Notice that tusks on a baby animal should always be small.

HUGE EARS

It's cute to draw a "cape" of ears that hangs behind the elephant.

Monkeying Around

Young monkeys have a bright-eyed, curious look. They have very small bodies and short legs, with extremely long arms, large hands, and long fingers. The forehead is always large, usually with thick eyebrows. Draw wide, funny ears and a long, curving tail.

Primate Primer

Even though primates have a lot in common, the chimpanzee is *not* all that similar to the powerful gorilla. Gorillas have wide necks and shoulders. Chimps have small shoulders and skinny necks (or no neck).

TYPICAL MONKEY STANCE
Monkeys rest on the backs of their hands, not on the palms.

Use a single line to draw both eyebrows.

Keep the chin small but the upper lip long. Leave lots of space between the nose and upper lip.

Monkeys always have gangly arms.

Lions

Young lions don't have manes. Their heads look rather bony. To capture this feel, give your cub's face a kind of rounded-square shape.

Notice how wide the upper mouth area is.

Tigers

Think of tiger cubs as playful kittens with wider faces and stripes. Even the paws should be thick and round, like kitten paws. Be sure to add ruffles at the cheeks and long whiskers. And be bold—don't draw tiny stripes just because the cub is tiny.

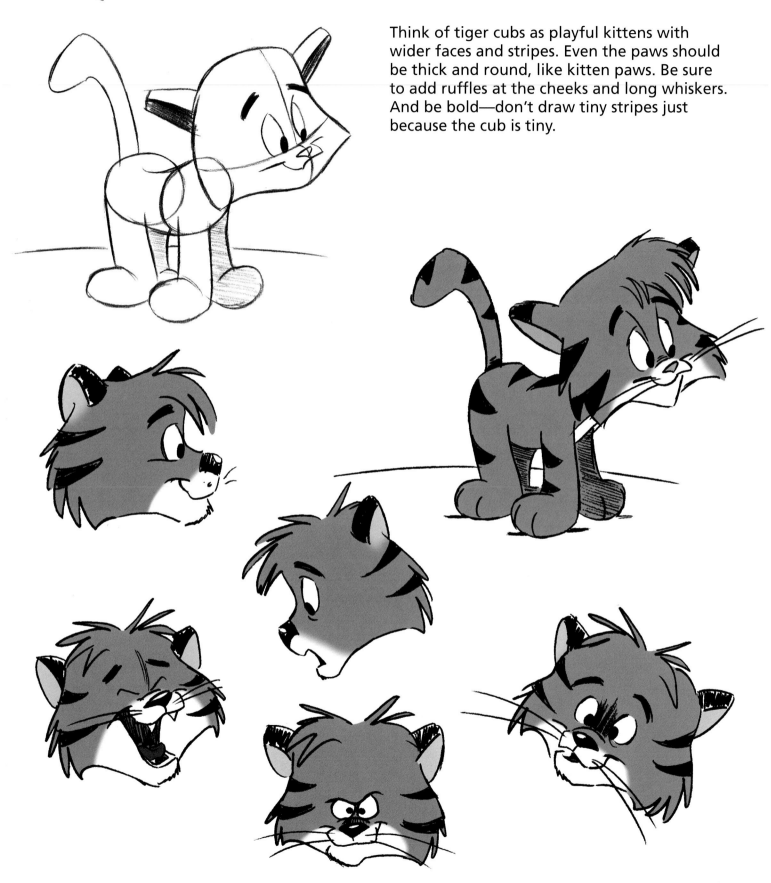

The far leg should always be shorter than the near one, due to perspective.

Some of the best-loved and funniest baby animals are the chubby ones. Hippopotamus babies are one example. While the bodies of thin animals are usually drawn with two overlapping circles (like the tiger on page 32), heavy baby animals are made from one single shape.

Rhinos

There are two types of rhinoceros. The Asian rhino looks like it's wearing "armor plates." The African rhino has smoother skin. Remember to make the horn on a young rhino small.

The snout forms a long, curving line.

A rhino's upper lip hangs over its bottom one.

THE RHINOCEROS HEAD
The rhino's face is long and narrow. But in cartoons you can also make it short and wide, as I've done here.

CHARGE!

To draw the "armor plates" of an Asian rhino, divide its body into three sections.

Giraffes

Giraffes are built very oddly. They have long necks, a hump at their shoulders, and short bodies.

MOTHERS AND THEIR YOUNG
Wherever there's a baby animal, there's a mother close behind. Animal moms are fierce defenders of their young, always keeping a watchful eye.

Zebras

Yep, they're striped horses—but not exactly. The zebra head is shorter and wider than that of the horse. Its mane sticks up like a mohawk. And the tail starts out like a skinny stick, with loose hair at the end. Always be sure to draw the stripes in the right direction. They go the short way around the body, not the long way.

LIKE THIS

NOT THIS

Bears

Bear cubs are everyone's favorites! They should be round and chubby, with fat cheeks, big paws, and cute tummies that stick out a little. Add a tuft of hair at the top of the forehead.

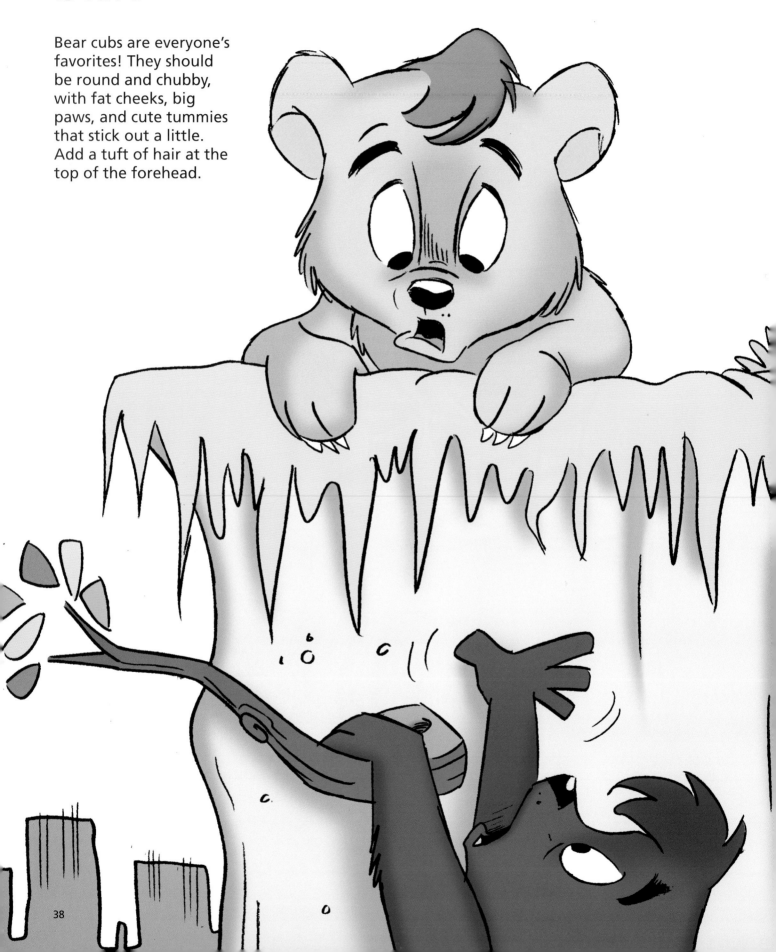

Panda Bears

Pandas munch all day on bamboo. They are a little shorter and fatter than brown bears, but it's their black-and-white markings that really make them look different.

SEA CREATURES AND REPTILES

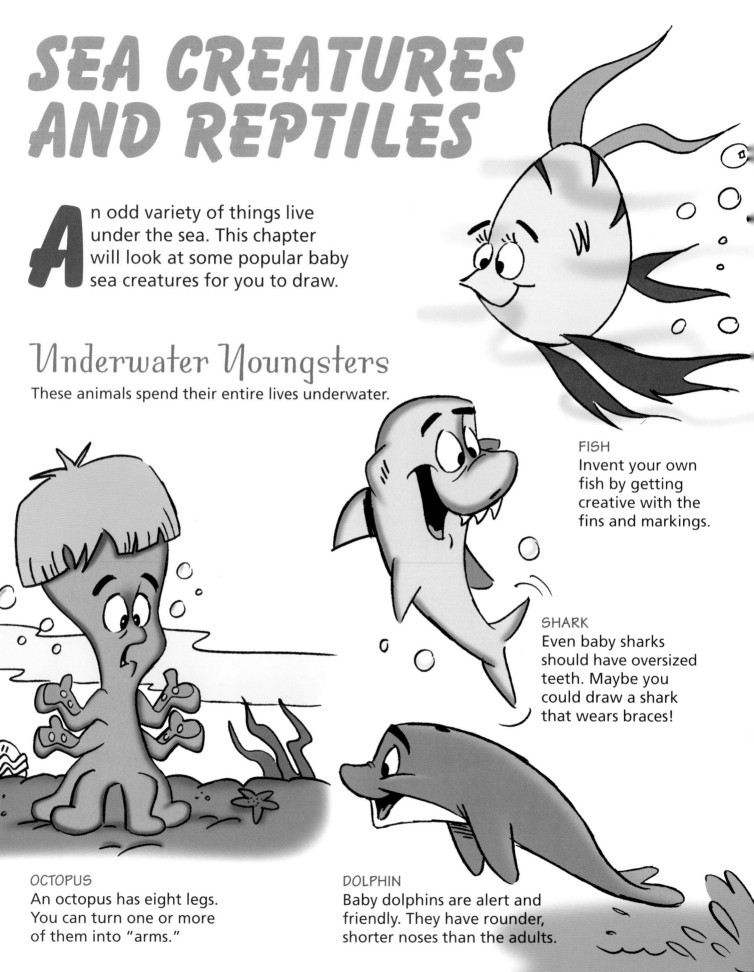

An odd variety of things live under the sea. This chapter will look at some popular baby sea creatures for you to draw.

Underwater Youngsters

These animals spend their entire lives underwater.

FISH
Invent your own fish by getting creative with the fins and markings.

SHARK
Even baby sharks should have oversized teeth. Maybe you could draw a shark that wears braces!

OCTOPUS
An octopus has eight legs. You can turn one or more of them into "arms."

DOLPHIN
Baby dolphins are alert and friendly. They have rounder, shorter noses than the adults.

Seals and Walruses

Take a look at the head of a seal. Now imagine it with long, floppy ears. What does it remind you of? If you thought of a dog, you're right. The shape of a seal's head is like that of a puppy, but without the long ears—and with extra whiskers.

The walrus pup, on the other hand, is much plumper and has a rounder head. Its tusks are small.

A Whale of a Baby

Even the biggest creatures start out small—if you can call something the size of a truck small! To draw a baby whale, keep the head large but shorten the length of the body. The head should be very wide, and the eyes bigger than in real life.

Alligators

You can draw the nose of a baby alligator extra wide to make it look goofy and cute. Also, place the eyes close together.

Turtles, Snakes, and Frogs

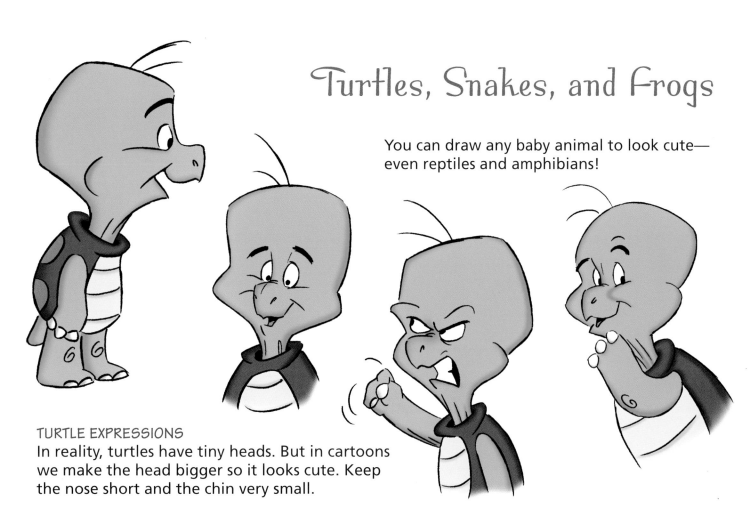

You can draw any baby animal to look cute—
even reptiles and amphibians!

TURTLE EXPRESSIONS
In reality, turtles have tiny heads. But in cartoons
we make the head bigger so it looks cute. Keep
the nose short and the chin very small.

GOOFY VS. ADORABLE
Reptiles (and amphibians)
are a little "weird looking"
as compared to, say, puppies.
So it's better to make them
look goofy than adorable.
Adorable is too much of
a stretch for most reptiles!

SMALL CUTIES

ere are a few small rascals to add to your bag of tricks.

Basic Little Birds

Little birds should have large heads and small bodies. Make the legs tiny and the eyes big.

1

2

3

4

HOW THE WING FOLDS

Ever want to know how a bird's wing folds in on itself? Well, you've come to the right place.

Penguins (Brr!)

When a mother penguin lays an egg, the father protects the egg from the cold by standing in freezing temperatures for weeks, guarding it with his warm body while the mother goes off for a long swim. Who do you think got the better deal here?

When drawing a baby penguin, make sure the shoulders are slightly hunched, with no neck at all. The legs are very short but the feet are big. All penguins are plump. They need the fat to protect them from the harsh weather.

Ducks

Ducklings waddle along with huge heads that teeter on small bodies. Their immature beaks are short and round. I gave this duckling long eyelashes to help it look young.

DUCKLING

Notice the difference in head size between the adult and the baby.

ADULT DUCK

This father and son pair of beavers are about to eagerly take on a task. And no doubt, it will be exhausting to watch them! Note that the father has two huge teeth, but the son has only one. Also, the younger beaver has a larger forehead and more hair than the adult.

Pig-out!

Piglets have short but large snouts, large ears, and corkscrew tails. They have round bodies and no neck—just place the head right on the shoulders.

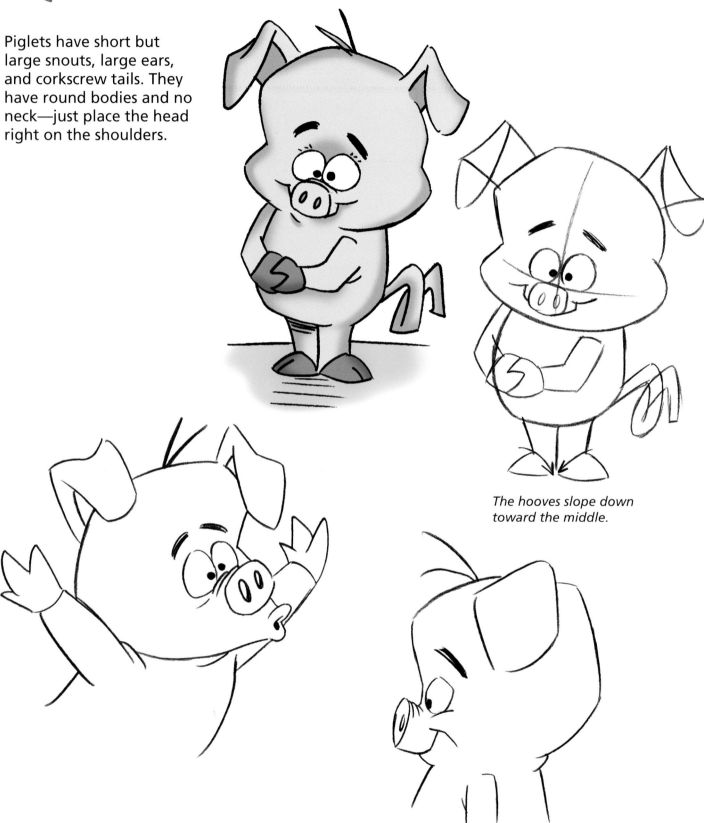

The hooves slope down toward the middle.

HUNGRY PIG
Hey, he didn't get that
way by eating salad!

HOUSE PETS AND PESTS

What's the difference between a pet and a pest? If your mom shrieks when she sees one in the house, it's a pest.

Bunnies

Bunnies are the ultimate warm and fuzzy pet.

CUTE 'N' FLUFFY
This bunny's head has two parts: the forehead section and the mouth section. The ears are short and wide. The paws are softer and plumper than on the grumpy rabbit.

GRUMPY
Even the whiskers on this bunny seem grumpy! Notice that this time the head has just one overall shape.

RABBITS 4
TORTOISES 3

PLAY BALL!
Invent new bunny characters
by making the head wider
or thinner, making the body
skinny or fat, or changing
the shape of the ears.

Bunnies in Motion: Bunching and Stretching

When a bunny leaps forward, it starts by coiling up like a spring. Its body *bunches* up and becomes shorter. As it springs forward, it *stretches* and gets longer. Then it bunches up again when it hits the ground.

| COIL (BUNCH) | SPRING (STRETCH) | LEAP (STRETCH) | LAND (BUNCH) |

How Much Is That Doggy in the Window?

Puppies have all the key qualities that make for cute baby animals: floppy ears, shaggy hair, short tails, big eyes, and tiny mouths.

Purebred Puppies

COCKER SPANIEL

Cocker spaniels have sweet personalities, gentle eyes, and long flowing ears. They should look well groomed—as if their owners lived in expensive apartment buildings in New York City.

OLD ENGLISH SHEEPDOG

He's got eyes, but you'd never know it by looking at him! Notice the shaggy upper lip and paws, and the short tail.

POODLE

What is it with poodle owners? Do they really think those haircuts look good? These smart little puppies should always look pampered. Draw the ears extra long and add big curly poufs of hair.

BULL TERRIER

The bull terrier is a funny-looking dog. It has pointy ears and facial features that are close together on a large head. Its body is muscular, but somehow it still looks a bit pudgy.

BLOODHOUND

This droopy puppy has long floppy ears, a wrinkled forehead, and long flews (upper lip flaps). It has a long body with loose skin and big paws.

Mutts, Mutts, and More Mutts!

Any dog that is not a special breed is a mutt. Mutts are fun to draw because there are no rules—you can create any kind you want. In cartoons, mutts are usually city dogs who survive on the streets by using their wits.

Cute Little Fur Balls

Why is it that everyone loves kittens? Kittens are famous for their big eyes, oversized paws, and plump bodies. They also have short snouts and small mouths and chins. How can something so cute be so bad for your allergies?

Hints for Drawing Kittens

SITTING KITTENS
When a kitten sits, its knees rest on the tops of its hind paws, hiding them from view.

HIND PAWS ARE COMPLETELY HIDDEN

SIDE VIEW
In the side view, only part of the rear paws are hidden.

There are three major bones in the kitten's leg, although you may not see them all in certain positions.

PAWS
A relaxed front paw curves upward, not downward.

RIGHT

WRONG

Mice

MISCHIEVOUS HOUSE MOUSE
The cartoon mouse usually walks upright on two legs and has a very large head, bushy cheeks, and huge ears. The feet are incredibly long compared to the rest of the body.

SHY HOUSE MOUSE

This little character is more like a "real" mouse. Large eyes and some hair help make it look cute.

INDEX

action line, 8
alligators, 44
amphibians, 45
anatomy, 12
awkward baby, 13

bears
    body, 8-9, 10, 11
    head, 6–7, 11
    pandas, 39
    paws, 16
    ruffles of fur, 22, 23
    sitting, 11
    standing upright, 8, 10
beavers, 49
birds
    basic, 46
    ducks, 48
    penguins, 47
bloodhounds, 58
body
    action line, 8
    baby vs. adult, 14, 15
    bone structure, 12
    draw-through, 10
    heavy vs. thin, 33
    proportions, 14
    side view, 9
    3/4 view, 9
    traits of baby, 15
    See also name of animal
bratty baby, 13
bull terriers, 58
bunching, 21, 54
bunnies. *See* rabbits

camels, 16
cats, 22, 60–61
centerline, 6
cheeks, 7, 21
    ruffles of fur, 22, 23
chin, 21
claws, 11
cocker spaniels, 56
crocodiles, 44
curious expression, 25
cuteness, 44, 52, 55

deer, 16
dogs
    breeds, 56–58
    cuteness, 55
    mutts, 59
    paws, 16
    ruffles of fur, 22
dolphins, 40
draw-through, 10
dreamy expression, 25
ducks, 48

elephants, 16, 26–28
evil baby, 13

eyes
    in perspective, 17
    placement of, 6, 19

face mask, 10
facial expressions, 24–25, 52, 62–63
father and son, 49
fish, 40
forehead, 6, 18
frogs, 45
fur, ruffles of, 22–23

genius baby, 13
giant baby, 13
giraffes, 16, 36
goofy baby, 13, 44, 45
gorilla, 30
grossed out expression, 25
grumpy expression, 52

head
    back of, 19
    eyes, 6, 17, 19
    face mask, 10
    facial expressions, 24–25, 52, 62–63
    forehead, 6, 18
    mouth, 21
    muzzle, 20
    placement of features, 6
    3/4 view, 7, 9
    See also name of animal
hippos, 16, 33
horses, 12, 13, 14, 16

joyful expression, 24

kittens, 22, 60-61

laughing expression, 24

leaping, 54
leggy baby, 13
leopards, 16
lions, 31

mice, 62–63
mischievous expression, 24, 62
monkeys, 16, 29–30
mothers and young, 36
mouth, 21
muzzle, 6, 20

neck, 6
newborns, 6

octopus, 40
old English sheepdogs, 56

panda bears, 39
paws, 11, 16
penguins, 47
personality, types of, 13
pigs, 19, 50–51
poodles, 57
posture, 15
proportions, 14
puppies. *See* dogs

rabbits
    body, 12, 53
    facial expressions, 13, 52
    in motion, 54
reptiles, 45
rhinos, 16, 34–35

sad expression, 25
seals, 41
sharks, 40
sheepdogs, old English, 56
shy expression, 63
side view, 9
sitting, 11, 61
smile, 7
snakes, 45
snout, 7, 38
squashing, 21
standing upright, 10
stretching, 21, 54
surprised expression, 21, 24

teeth, 21
3/4 view, 7, 9
tigers, 22, 32
turtles, 45

underwater babies, 40, 42

walruses, 41
warm and fuzzy baby, 13
whales, 42–43
wings, folded, 46
wolves, 21